The P

by Lynn Edwards

illustrated by Kersti Frigell

SRA McGraw-Hill

Columbus, Ohio

A Division of The McGraw·Hill Companies

SRA/McGraw-Hill

A Division of The **McGraw·Hill** *Companies*

Printed in the United States of America.

Send all inquiries to:
SRA/McGraw-Hill
250 Old Wilson Bridge Road
Suite 310
Worthington, OH 43085

ISBN 0-02-674286-1
 2 3 4 5 6 7 8 9 SEG 00 99 98 97

the trees

3

the children

the 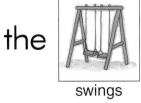 swings

the

slide

the
sandbox

7

the park